Challenges of Christian Marriage In African Culture

Challenges of Christian Marriage In African Culture

Sylvester Oyeka

authorHOUSE®

AuthorHouse™ UK
1663 Liberty Drive
Bloomington, IN 47403 USA
www.authorhouse.co.uk
Phone: 0800.197.4150

Published by AuthorHouse 09/22/2015

ISBN: 978-1-5049-4693-3 (sc)
ISBN: 978-1-5049-4694-0 (hc)
ISBN: 978-1-5049-4695-7 (e)

Print information available on the last page.

Table of Contents

Abstract

This Book aims at a comparative analysis between the African traditional marriage and the Christian marriage in order to extract some qualities which are universally accepted in creating a sustainable marriage. In order to achieve this, the Book explores the different concepts of marriage between the two traditions. In the course of this exploration marriage in Africa is seen as an ancestral vocation geared towards the fulfillment of a social task of regenerating the community, which is the foundation of human growth and development. It therefore implies following the findings of this Book that entrance into marital life involves integration into the goals and aspirations of the community. Life in isolation is totally abhorred in this environment and thus for a social acceptance, one must be in solidarity with the community. The community is the base for human self realization. Furthermore in the course of the research Christian marriage is projected as a marriage that contradicts the communal idea of the Igbo traditional marriage. Christian sacred union therefore, is seen here as the awakening of consciousness, that marriage is not just a communal ritual, but a voluntary venture which ought to be undertaken freely by the couple involved without the compulsion of the community. This sacred union in the Christian perspective is a decision, spouses make based on love, which is sacrificial, selfless, enduring and demanding. The Christian marriage is a sacred union, which involves a symbiotic relationship between spouses rooted in a selfless and sacrificial love. Nevertheless in bringing the Christian marriage parallel to the African traditional marriage one discovers that, which makes the Christian marriage unique. This is the ability to resist the crisis of marriage which involves childlessness, poverty, and deteriorating health. Under these conditions the Christian marriage demonstrates infinite patience. In view of this analysis this Book, projects love, infinite patience and selflessness as factors needed for sustainable marriage, which can be universally applicable, and recommends symbiotic relationship between spouses which is enabled by communication. Communication in marriage is generally emphasized in this project as stepping stone towards the couple's understanding of each other. However this Book may not resolve all the problems in marriage perfectly, since it cannot give adequate account of the study of human temperaments which are witnessed in every marriage because of the limited number of pages stipulated for this Book. It therefore opens way for more researches that explore the other aspects in marriage that hinder a sustainable marriage.

Chapter One

General Introduction

1.1 MARRIAGE IN AFRICA WORLDVIEW

Among the significant events in the Africa culture, marriage seems to be the most prominent event. This lies on the fact that human family is established through marriage and through the family a community is built. Owing to this importance attached to marriage as the building block of the community, marriage assumes its social task. The marriage bond ties together the couple from which the future members of the family must come.

Obviously, a family is not formed until all the marriage customs are fulfilled. In addition a marriage is not valid in an Africa cultural setting, until it is endorsed by the fruit of the womb. The absence of the fruit of the womb is often associated to curse and that is seen an evidence of an unapproved marriage by God and the ancestors. However, marriage is not an affair of one man and one woman as no one is an island, on this ground the man and the woman ought to be attentive to the community for a better discernment and approval of marriage. The family is the procreator of lives and this is only established through marriage and no community will remain if no procreation of lives is achieved, for this marriage must be safe guarded by the community under the influence of the ancestors.

The principle that dictates the choice of a marriage partner is based on an Africa love for children. Hence, this selection, which deals with the precious element of man, is entrusted to the community, and to the ancestors who stand as effective mediators between God and humanity. In choosing a marriage partner therefore, a man is aware of the fact that he is taking a decision to bring a new life and a new existence into the family and into his community of beings.

1.2 MARRIAGE IN CHRISTIAN WORLDVIEW

Nevertheless, Christianity has a different perception of marriage. Here, marriage shifts from a community imposition and assumes the role of personal commitment and sacrifice freely undertaken. The man and the woman consciously make a selection of each other based on love for each other as the primary factor and for the procreation of children if God wills. The existence of this marriage in an Igbo culture, where marriage is communitarian becomes threatened by cultural factors. How can this marriage based on love survive where emphasis is laid on child bearing and community supervision? This marriage is unrealizable for an African man unless it is endorsed by the fruit of the womb and kept under the strict supervision of kindred and community in solidarity with the ancestors. Hence in this environment the Christian marriage becomes threatened.

1.3 THE CONTRAST BETWEEN AFRICAN MARRIAGE AND CHRISTIAN MARRIAGE A CHALLENGE

The contrary views shared by Christianity and African culture with regard to marriage have often posed tremendous problem to the African Christian marriage. Marriage is often seen as a communal affair in the African cultural setting and aims towards the procreation of children since life is that which validates marriage. The decision of the African marriage is not dependent on the couple but on the community, which sees it as her task, since marriage initiates the family which is the fundamental unit of the community. The desire of the immortality of the community empowers the community to dictate on the issue of marriage.

However, Christian orientation differs in this regard. This is obviously because marriage is seen as a conscious decision of the couple based on love which is founded on Christ, the author of the Christian faith. The platform for Christian marriage is love and procreation becomes the fruit of this love. But the problem becomes more critical when determining how this Christian marriage can survive in an Igbo environment with a different philosophy of life.

It is important to mention here the father-son relationship. This relationship is crucial to the traditional system and affects every marriage. It is the basis of ancestral authority upon which the continuity of the institutions, values, attitudes and sentiments of Igbo culture depend. Christian marriage, in which a couple takes an independent position, becomes threatened in this culture where authority is centered on the community. Hence Christian marriage continues to be a rivalry to the community, in which marriage must be kept under its strict vigilance, Edeh (1985:58).

1.4 FUNDAMENTAL ELEMENT OF MARRIAGE

Love is that which must be cherished in every marriage for it to endure the challenges of life. Man should be aware that the only force that sustains a companionship is love. Hence this force love is what should be pursued in every union that involves a man and a woman. This Book aims therefore to re-orientate the African community that love is that which must be pursued in every marriage, hence procreation of children must not take precedence since love based on this is conditional and does not endure the challenges of time.

Furthermore, this Book projects marriage where a couple should be allowed to make a voluntary decision on their marriage and to be exposed to that love which is fundamental to every marriage. The procreation of children must be seen as the fruit of this sacred love and must be seen as the gift of God that brings the marriage to a consummation.

1.5 SIGNIFICANCE OF THIS BOOK

The Book serves as a mind opener to a new perspective of life. It is an enlightenment of the mind that true love is the only tool necessary for a sustainable marriage. Marriage is that, which can only be created through a free will not by compulsion.

However, this project is a conscious effort to teach a community to look into that, which endures in every marriage. It is a call for a reflection on personal responsibility to love. This responsibility is not imposed by the community or kindred but voluntarily taken up by the partners in marriage. It aims at enlightening the Igboman that life is beyond the perceptible.

1.6 SCOPE OF THIS BOOK

This Book takes its root from Igbo cultural settings and attempts at reflecting on the Igbo perspective of marriage, relating it to Christian perspective in order to make a possible evaluation. In this relationship the Christianity which is situated in African land is challenged considering the diverse ways in which marriage is perceived.

Nevertheless there can be some extensive study beyond the Igbo culture as the Book proceeds, but this will revolve round Africa in the course of the general views of marriage. The Igbo idea of marriage could be tackled revolving round Africa in order to extract some ideas which can be seen as unifying factors, acting as threat to the Christian marriage in African and the Igbo nation.

Chapter Two

What Actually is Marriage?

2.1 MARRIAGE

There is no definition that can actually exhaust the concepts of marriage. The understanding of marriage is an ongoing one. The meaning of marriages in a transition from one generation to the other is often encountered with the problem of differences in ideas. Marriage in itself is broader than the surface understanding; this is why it is often misunderstood and suffers a lot of challenges. In my own conception marriage could be seen as a vocation of love which opposite partners freely and consciously undertake in order to enjoy an intimate relationship between each other made visible by the procreation of a new life. In other words it is a union of a man and a woman under the umbrella of love, which aims at procreation.

Marriage in its sacramental structure is a physical manifestation of God's love for man which led to creation. In this perspective of sacramentality the code of canon Law 1012 puts it; "Christ our Lord elevated the matrimonial contract between two baptized persons to the dignity of a sacrament". In view of the above analysis every marriage is understood from a particular perspective.

Nevertheless, marriage could be seen as both communitarian and individual responsibility. As communitarian it is not a decision of the couple alone, it is a decision approved by the community that sees marriage as the fundamental units that generates a family, which is the fundamental unity of the community. However, these two perspectives of marriage; the communitarian and individualistic could be seen in the course of the project.

2.2 WHAT REALLY IS CHRISTIAN MARRIAGE?

The Christian marriage is a representation of the love that exists between Christ and the church (Eph 5:32). Hence the Vatican II council encourages that the Christian marriage should recognize the greater excellence of virginity consecrated to Christ so as to offer body and soul completely to God (*Decree on the Training of Priests N.9*).

Furthermore, the catechism of the Catholic Church 1601 defines marriage as an establishment geared towards a whole life partnership ordered towards the good of the spouses and the procreation and education of offspring. In this analysis one discovers the two significant elements of a Christian marriage. These include the good of the partners involved in the marriage. This involves the experience of the fullness of love; a reflection of the love Christ has for the whole world. Secondly, one sees the procreation of children as the fruit of this love. In view of these analyses, Christian marriage can be defined as an establishment of partnership between a man and a woman in conformity with love of Christ, exhibited to the church for the purpose of the procreation of children if God wills and for the education of the offspring.

2.3 THE IGBO CONCEPT OF MARRIAGE

Marriage in Igbo implies a communitarian vocation for the continuity of life, through establishment of partnership approved by the community. This practice is not an individual responsibility, it must be in concordance to the will of the community, and hence no marriage is contracted when left on the personal decision of the young couple. The insistence on a personal decision on marriage brings about a denial of the parental blessing.

The Igbo marriage is much more group oriented than the Christian marriage. This is because the marriage of one African affects his or her descent group so profoundly, the group is likely to take much greater interest in the choice of a spouse, and exercise much more control and limitation upon the choice of a partner.

Chapter Three

Different Perspectives of Marriage

The concept of marriage has been an issue of great concern to many theologians. The obvious reason for this inquisitive attitude towards marriage is because of its relevance as the fundamental unit of any society. Just as the human cell is the fundamental unit of life so also is marriage the fundamental unit of any society. Hence when marriage is contracted, the regeneration of a society is proposed and when a family is established a new society is formed. Marriage can be seen in the perspective of these different authors and theologians.

Nevertheless, in studying the views of theologians and sociologists on marriage we discover that marriage is seen as a social task. Marriage as a social task is seen as responsibility one fulfils for the society in bringing new life to the community. When we move further we see marriage discussed in the perspective of companionship, marriage in this perspective becomes a mutual sharing of the partners involved. Moreover, some see marriage as a vocation of the ancestors and hence it becomes the responsibility of such ancestor to safeguard marriage, then marriage as transformational. Marriage could also be seen as that union, whose goal is towards procreation.

Finally, marriage shall be discussed in the sense of being a sacrament. In this sense marriage is regarded as a symbol which portrays a sharing of being or an enactment of love which is a reflection of the love Christ has for the world. Under these categories we shall be able to represent the views of different theologians and these steps act as stepping stones towards the real meaning of marriage.

Schillbeeckx is one among the theologians that view marriage as a social task. Hence in his book; Marriage human reality, describes marriage in the traditional setting as an entrance into a pre-arranged social entity, a working community which more or less coincided with the extended, Schillebeekx (1965). The implication of this is that marriage cannot stand outside the society; hence marriage becomes integration into the social order where the couples become agents of this social task. Schillebeeks went to elucidate this by a claim that married life and the families were supported by society, though the personal and subjective sides of marriage were present but silent and inconspicuous.

Furthermore, L. Roussel describes marriage as a gateway towards the acquisition of social status in his book "*Le Marriage Dan La Societe Francaise*". He writes from this book that marriage is the most excellent act through which one becomes recognized member of a society. Hence it alone was the basis for the legitimacy of children and determines the social basis in which he can interact.

It becomes obvious from this analysis that marriage has a social significance. This is because it is not just an individual venture, but an act which integrates one to the large community and gives one a social identity through which he can exercise his freedom with the state social affairs.

Moreover, among the Igbo, marriage events are regarded highly. Marriage takes its meaning within the community; every marriage is integration into the community of the actualized and acquisition of full right to participate in community's affairs. This implies that an unmarried person is a nonentity. Marriage in this situation could also be seen as an adult task, imposed on individual on the ground that they are members of the community and exist within it. In the course of this undertaken individuals incorporate themselves into the larger community and form a network of new relationship, Agbasiere (2000:94).

In this principle of communitarian accordance of importance to marriage, a man or a woman is not recognized in the Igbo community unless he or she is married. This is the obvious reason why a woman does not belong to Umuada group unless she is married. One begins to ask, does it mean before the marital state the man or woman lacks his or her rationality as an individual? A man is never counted as a distinct individual unless he is married or else he is recognized through his father. The consequence of this ideology is that if a man fails to marry he is called an irresponsible man. This is because marriage is seen as a task not as an individual task but as a social task, which all must participate to ensure the immortality of the community.

An unmarried man is a shame to his father, an enemy to community regeneration. Every marriage among the Igbo is seen as a vocation to the community; hence all must be alert to respond to this precious vocation. The Igbo for Agbasiere, strongly believes that existence for any human being is not fortuitous and that life belongs to the creator. Hence the goal of life is seen as marriage and procreation of children for the lineage and for the ancestors and this is assumed to be the greatest goal and the most significant ritual act of human existence. The implication of this according to Agbasiere is that humanity is defined in relationship to marriage, that is, one ought to wait for the attainment of marriage age before he or she will be recognized as a human person.

The Catholic Church never remained silent on issues concerning marriage. Marriage is seen as a process of companionship founded on the love of Christ consummated in procreation. Hence, Canon 1055 rightly puts it;

> The matrimonial covenant by which a man and a woman establish between themselves a partnership of the whole life, is by its nature ordered towards the good of the spouses and the procreation and education of offspring.

This implies that companionship must not be separated from marriage even though it is directed towards the procreation of children. The canon moves further to establish a ground for indissolubility of marriage and in this the Christian marriage which is characterized by firmness is established (Canon 1056).

Nevertheless, the choice of partners should be a free act of people who are capable of reasoning and deemed matured by law to giving consent. This implies that the definition of Christian marriage is; a life partnership freely chosen by two people considered matured by law, to re-enact the love Christ exhibited to the world, aim at procreation of children in the light of Christian faith.

In this definition of Christian marriage the three essential factors are; freedom, maturity and love. These three factors are necessary for the validity of Christian marriage; nevertheless, self acceptance is seen as a significant condition for marriage, since through this an unconditional and sacrificial marriage is established.

Moreover, Calderone (1988) defines marriage as a form of symbiotic relationship between spouses, equal in human dignity, which involves companionship and the sharing of each other's being. Thus marriage is described here as a means of living together, growing together, building a relationship that is a source of strength for two people, not only a refuge from the world for them but also a springboard into the world. In this type of relationship one sees the other as the most important person in the world, through this a sustainable existence is established which can lead to sexual relationship.

Clayton C. Barbeau views marriage from a relational perspective; for him marriage is an establishment of a mutual relationship, whereby roles are shared between the partners for the benefit of the established family, without diminishing the personality and dignity of any of spouses involve in the relationship, Calderone (1989). In this type of relationship, each partner sees himself or herself as a gift to the other. In this relational perspective marriage is founded on a symbiotic relationship, here each partner sees himself or herself as a complement to the other. Hence roles are shared not for any reason based on subordination but for the convenience of the partners who willingly come together. The fundamental reason behind this relational perspective of marriage which calls for a symbiotic relationship is that the home belongs to both partners; therefore it is their shared responsibility to ensure its sustenance.

Pierre (1987) reacted against those who saw marriage as directed only toward procreation. For him he considers the relationship between the couple as necessary to sustain marriage. Hence couple finds fulfillment in this mutual sharing of one another. Thus Pierre describes marriage as a vocation of humanity which involves the sharing of being; a companionship where spouses are gifts to one another for emotional and psychological development; that is being for the other, called to find life through the other, and through the other he is fertile. In this way he responds to God's call.

Furthermore, in Africa the ancestors occupy eminent positions in the life of the living. The ancestors serve as custodians both to morality and norms that guide the life of individuals. Events like marriages become the responsibility of the ancestors for endorsement and continuous guide, hence a marriage without the endorsement or approval of the ancestors becomes like a man chasing the wind. Among the Urhobo people marriage is seen as a significant event which is approved and guarded by the ancestors. This implies that there is no marriage in Urhobo that is regarded as properly contracted without the offering of drinks to the ancestors. This acceptance of drinks by the ancestor is an indication of the approval of the marriage known as Udi Arhovbaje (acceptance drink). This takes place in the ancestral shrine of the girl, Adegbola (1983:313).

Obviously, in this cultural setting where marriage is seen as a response to the call of the ancestor, for every marriage to be valid, it must be approved by the ancestors, who remain the custodians of the marriage. Marriage here is seen as a cultural heritage; hence it must receive its social status from the ancestors who are the invisible cultural custodians of social norms.

Nevertheless, marriage in itself is mysterious; this is because its meaning cannot be totally exhausted. The meaning of marriage is not static; it therefore continues to generate different meanings to humanity at every stage as a result of human varied experiences of life; this is why an infant cannot go into marriage. The issue of marriage is very complicated hence, marriage could be seen in different perspectives, its meaning remains transformational; as one moves from one age to the other his or her understanding of marriage continues to experience transformation. One begins to move from the illusory understanding of marriage to the real understanding of marriage when one is being exposed to the conditions of life. The world is not a bed of roses neither is the world a bed of thorns; this adage portrays the condition of marriage which can only be understood at a particular stage in life.

James Gretema (1993:13) dwells on this transformational perspective of marriage. Hence, for him marriage is seen as a relationship involving two different individuals, which passes different stages of understanding from the level of emotionality or illusion to the level of reality or reason. It could be deduced from James description of marriage that marriage is always in the process of development, just as a child passes from infancy to adulthood. Hence in marriage, the individuals first embrace each other based on some elements of illusions. But when the two partners are exposed to the realities of life which consists of up and down, the meaning of marriage for the couple begins to change. At this stage each begins to understand the other as a burden which one is committed to and the mind begins to reconstruct itself towards the acceptance of the other which must be accommodated. This period of understanding characterized by transformation of marriage understanding is often being experienced by conflict and resolution.

Nevertheless, this process of development is a transition from illusion to disillusion, immaturity to a level of maturity, emotion to reason and appearance to reality. It is a gradual climbing towards the understanding of that which is surrounded by obscurity. In this gradual climbing one renounces himself or herself in order to understand the being of the other, so as to commit his or her life to the other amidst the up and down of life.

Nevertheless, marriage remains a great event whose meaning can never be exhausted. The meaning of marriage continues to unravel in one's life time; hence one takes his or her whole earthly existence to understanding the principle of marriage. However, some undermine the relational pleasure in marriage and view marriage as a union which partners engage on, not for emotional satisfaction but for the desire to bring new life to the world.

Hence, in this understanding marriage is seen as performing the task of procreation. St Augustine adopted this idea, for the bishop of Hippo marriage is seen in the perspective of fulfilling procreative responsibility. In this Augustine developed a theory demonstrating that matrimonial union, though polluted by physical desire finds a value in submitting itself to a superior end: procreation. By projecting the procreative role of marriage as the basis for its establishment, Augustine wished to condemn the encroachment of sexual passion and pleasure which for him has polluted this sacred union. With regard to polygamy Augustine asserted that he has no problem with it and claimed that it is neither against nature nor reason. In this the Bishop of Hippo posited that the important thing in marriage is mutual love, education of children and peace in the family, Arazu (1994).

When one maintains the position of St Augustine, marital life could only be seen in terms of conjugal duty, this implies that marriage could only be endorsed by the arrival of children. The question lying here is what becomes of the man and the woman beside the primary task of procreation? If marriage ends in procreation it therefore implies that the relationship of the man and the woman is centered on this procreation.

Nevertheless, marriage in itself is symbolic, in this line of thought maintains its sacramental quality. Benezeri in his book; African Christian marriage discusses the sacramentality of marriage, which for him was posited by Peter Louis. By positing marriage as a sacrament Peter attempts at projecting the effective sign value of marriage as it is understood by Christians. Fundamentally, marriage is called a sacrament because it is part of created order. It is divinely instituted by mere creation of male and female which are complementary in nature. To be candid, sacramental thinking is the characteristic form of a person's first thinking about reality. Marriage itself is symbolic and form part of the most important event of human existence. It projects the love of God for humanity which is expressed in the love displayed by the co-existing partners.

The ceremonies and rituals with which people surround this event of marriage is an indication of the fact that it is in this situation that they experience the transcendent character of life and the divine origin and goal of their existence. It is especially through this relationship that humanity is able to comprehend the love of God immanent in his creatures. God's love is sacramentally communicated in every human encounter, whether it is interpersonal, group or inter group, and people are called to respond to that love through relationship. Marriage becomes an avenue of expressing this divine love according to Peters Louis.

It therefore becomes necessary to place marriage as a symbol of God's unfailing love. Marriage is relational and God relates to us in our daily activities. Marriage is bind by commitment just as God is committed to us even by sharing his life with us. Marriage as sacramental becomes way of projecting these hidden values of marriage. These values include love, mutual commitment, sacrifice and mutual sharing.

In view of all these conceptions of marriage by different authors and cultures, one discovers that the meaning of marriage cannot be thoroughly exhausted. Marriage means different things for different people of different ages and worldviews. For a child marriage is seen as an exercise of freedom from the dictatorship of parents in order to exist independently as free individuals with full right of procreation. For the youth marriage is an enactment of love to one whom one deems appropriate for companionship in life.

However, the meaning of marriage changes, as one advances in age. Elderly men and women have different conceptions about marriage, for them who have experienced the up and down of life marriage becomes a sacrificial commitment with the other undermining the up and down of life. This ideological difference between the youth and elders is an indication that as one advances in age, the definition of marriage changes from illusion to the reality of life. The youths see marriage as a romantic display but for the old it is more of a sacrifice and self commitment. In every sacrifice one is faced with the bitter aspect of life.

In commitment one remains firm in both the sorrowful and joyous part of life. In romance one suppresses the reality of life and dwells in the world of emotion and illusion, stimulated by spontaneous pleasure without an insight of the future. Nevertheless, in any case marriage is a call to companionship amidst the strength and weaknesses of either partner.

Chapter Four

The Christian Marriage in an African (Igbo) Culture

4.1 THE CONCEPT OF MARRIAGE AMONG THE IGBO

The encroachment of Christianity into a pre-existent Igbo culture has brought in with it, a radical change in the perception of things. The two ways of life have been in conflict over the years; looking for ways of arriving at a reconciliation. Obviously, most of the time, the reconciliation of these diverse beliefs about life, becomes difficult, because of the different philosophies of life governing the different systems; Christianity and tradition.

Nevertheless, the issue at hand is marriage. Marriage is one, among the numerous rituals in the African land, which stands out as the building block of the community. Marriage in Igbo cultural setting has been viewed in diverse ways; some are seen as a social task, integration into the society with the primary goal of contributing to the regeneration of the society. The Igbo man places emphasis on child bearing and any marriage denied of this fruit of the womb is seen as a curse. Marriage is a vocation of the ancestor; hence any man who fails to respond to this vocation is termed irresponsible and unworthy to be reckoned as a man. Humanity is described in relationship to marriage.

Married life is the normal condition for the adult. It is an important status indicator for both women and men, since celibates are tolerated only as victims of unforeseen circumstances. The Igbo who remains single does so not voluntarily but because of his financial incapacity. The unmarried adult male is referred to as *oke okporo* which implies a male woman. This is a pejorative term. While the unmarried woman is referred to as *onweghi di* this implies she has no husband (Victor Uchendu, The Igbo of S.E Nigeria).

The journey to married life is the goal of the Igbo man. Marriage in Igbo land is a family responsibility where the parents to the couple in line with the kinsmen take initiative. It is a union of two communities; the community of the bride and that of the bridegroom. This unity is strengthened at the birth of a male child. Hence, marriage among the Igbo is that union between the people of the bride and the groom strengthened at the birth of a male child, Peil (1977).

In fact the family community is the fundamental element of the Africans, this provides platform for his action, outside this family support the individual remains a nonentity. In marriage, the man accepts the responsibility towards another family, Benezeri (1998). But no one goes into marriage alone; marriage preparation was a communitarian task. This communitarian responsibility attached to marriage gives rise to the popular Igbo adage; *otu onye anaghi alu nwanyi,* this means no man alone marries a wife; it is a joint responsibility between the man and the community. In any case the community must take precedence.

Marriage as integration into the vast community of relationship, confer in marriage great importance and relevance in the life of the people. Sequel to this importance attached to it, the whole community celebrates marriage rituals, and does these in varying ways, reflecting the communitarian character of customary marriage at family and community level.

4.2 PROCREATION: GOAL OF AFRICAN MARRIAGE

Procreation is strongly emphasized in Igbo cultural setting as condition that stabilizes a marriage. This is because of the consciousness of extinction of the family. Hence, childlessness is an indication of extinction which every Igbo man would like to avoid. In view of this polygamous marriage becomes the order of the day in search of heir of the family. Childlessness is not often tolerated, the sterile man is described as a woman in male form and the woman in turn is referred to as a man. The childless couple is often an object of mockery.

Moreover, one of the paramount aspirations of the community in the Igbo cultural setting is procreation as the ancestors recommended it. Thus, a man who dies without progeny falls into oblivion. This is unaccepted as the man fails to achieve the task of the ancestor. In some traditions, a piece of charcoal is put into his mouth to indicate that the fire of life had died out. In the researcher's community, Oraukwu in Anambra state, a man who dies unmarried is buried outside the living compound. It is seen as a curse to die without heir or progeny.

Procreation is thus a question not limited to individual survival but extended to the sustenance of the entire community. It therefore implies that extended family is assured by the marriage of its members a continuity of life, not any kind of marriage, but by the one, which bears fruit. Infertile couples for African mind are dead persons and as useless as dead wood.

Marriage is an ongoing process in Igbo land. For marriage to be completed it must be blessed with the fruit of the womb of both sexes. Male children are pride to their fathers because they stand as the possible heirs to their fathers and represent their fathers in community gathering. On the other hand, the female offsprings are flowers around their mothers. They assist their mothers in domestic works and provide resting places for their mothers when they get old, Benezet (1998:108).

4.3 EXTENDED FAMILY SYSTEM: CUSTODIAN OF AFRICAN MARRIAGE

African marriage in general has a strong communitarian character. In Igbo societies, a woman who is married enters the family community of her husband as a worker and bearer of children for the whole group. Her marriage is not bound to her husband, but in a very real sense to the group itself. She is the wife of the whole family and every member of the extended family of the husband, whether a man or a woman stands out as the husband. The woman identifies these members of the husband family as my husbands and she in turn becomes their wife.

Nevertheless, this does not, of course mean that any other male besides her husband has the right of sexual access to the woman, but it stresses her communitarian role and the range in which the woman can be protected by the kindred. A woman enjoys the security not only from the husband, but from the members of the extended family who call her "my wife". Hence this area of influence makes her very important and popular within the kindred of the husband.

The death of the husband of the woman is not the termination of the marriage. The marriage continues as long as the woman is married to the kindred of the man. Thus any of the brothers of the late husband has the right to take over the responsibility of the woman. In this arrangement, no bride price is being paid since it is a continuation of a marriage already contracted.

4.4 THE CHRISTIAN MARRIAGE

Christian marriage involves a life partnership of a man and a woman, who come together to share their beings together with the goal of the fruit of the womb. The Christian marriage brings men and women out of their isolation and alone-ness, so that they can complete or complement one another in a relationship of love. The unity which this marriage brings about is a mystery which defies the basic laws of Mathematics. In a simple equation one and one become two, but in this marriage one man and one woman develop a unity or oneness which results in two richer, deeper persons.

In the Christian perspective of marriage when a man and a woman give themselves in marriage Christ comes to dwell in their unity. The love which couple shares is the basis of Christian marriage and that is the principle behind its sustenance. This marriage is founded on the Genesis account: God created man and woman in his own image.

Man and woman are assigned an equal status by God at creation. In this relationship, sex is given a clearly defined role. This union which is experienced by these partners is the priority of Christian marriage and from this love emerges the fruit of the womb.

What makes Christian marriage distinct is that it is a contract entered freely and solemnly before God and man. The couple, by entering into this contract, set up a new relationship with their God with whom they cooperate to bring forth children, and with whose help they may return together. This relationship makes marriage not merely a contract but a sacrament and it is this sacramental aspect that makes a Christian marriage holy and distinct. This sacramental aspect of the Christian marriage makes it complicated for other people to comprehend. It cuts across all cultural sentiments and stands out on its own as unique and divinely established.

Not so long ago the prime purpose of marriage was seen to be the procreation and rearing of children, the weakness of this approach was that as everything was dependent on procreation it tended to devalue marriages in which no children were forthcoming. Fruitlessness does not destroy the substance and essence of Christian marriage as a sacrament which was instituted by God. In as much as a child is an expected fruit from the union of spouses in marriage, we must not equate it to the essence of marriage and see childlessness as a reason to nullify a marriage, except on the grounds that from the very beginning before the marriage, the spouses had reached an agreement that in the event of not having children they were going to separate or end the marriage. Reflecting on this the church deem it necessary to promote that relationship between the partners in marriage which is only triggered of by love. Hence, this relationship that exists between the husband and wife becomes the basis for Christian marriage.

The Christian marriage is established not primarily because of offspring but for the sake of those entering into union themselves. They depend on one another and share one another being. The primary task of a Christian marriage is the achievement of love which Christ expressed to his church. It is therefore, in this arena of love that God blesses the partners with the fruit of the womb. This implies that the fruit of the womb is not the primary target of the Christian marriage but a blessing for a union which is expressed in the symbiotic relationship of the husband and the wife.

In Christian marriage, man and woman must live together as one body. In this union oneness is expressed in the complementary roles of the two partners. The man needs the being of the woman just as the woman needs the being of the man. This relationship is more of mutuality and sharing at every level (Eph.5:21).

4.5 THE BIBLICAL FOUNDATION OF CHRISTIAN MARRIAGE

Christian marriage is described in the Epistle of St Paul as a symbiotic relationship between a man and a woman. Hence, in 1 Cor 7:13, St Paul asserts; the husband should give to his wife her conjugal rights and likewise, the wife to her husband. In first letter to the Corinthians (7:14) Paul says; for the unbelieving husband is consecrated through his wife and the unbelieving wife is consecrated through her husband. The biblical concept of marriage is that in marriage a new union of man and woman is established not only or even not primarily for the sake of offspring thereby, but for the sake of those entering into the relationship themselves. Christian marriage is a commitment which ought to be permanent; in this permanence it projects a sacrificial love between the man and the woman. Here Saint Paul asserts:

> “A wife must not be separated from her husband or if she has already left him, she must remain unmarried or else

to be reconciled to her husband, and a husband must not divorce his wife (1Cor 7:10-11)."

The Bible recognizes the dignity of both men and women. In marriage union this recognition of human values found in both male and female must not be taken for granted. Sex belongs to the man-woman relationship of marriage to the extent and depth that the two in reality and essence become one flesh. Here lies the mystery of human togetherness in marriage; a mystery applicable also to the unity between Christ and his Church (Eph 5:33).

Nevertheless, Christian marriage can take its structure from the relationship between Christ and the church even though that relationship presents an archetype which marriage can never perfectly resemble. Yet marriage can be lived psychologically within the rhythm of Christ's relations with the church, because in truth and reality Christian marriage exist only with the influence of Christ' universal love, reflecting in his marriage with the church.

Christian marriage is a sharing of one another being. In Galatians Paul repeats Christ's commandment: "out of Christian love place yourselves at one another service" (Gal 5:13). Here there is a demand to perform the office of a slave between the partners. By performing the offices of slave implies dying to one another, a mutual relationship which reflects the universal love of Christ. Submissiveness is the vocation of the Christian marriage. This submissiveness is symbiotic in the sense that it is expected from either partner. St Paul asserts; "submit to one another in fear of Christ".

Moreover, in Christian marriage the union of husband and wife means more than merely physical fruitfulness, the begetting of children, it means spiritual fruitfulness as well (Gal 5:22, Eph 5:9). Humanity comprises of both body and spirit. These combinations should be reflected in the marriage to achieve a Christian marriage, Demehy (1981).

4.6 COMPANIONSHIP IN LOVE: THE BASIS FOR CHRISTIAN MARRIAGE.

Marriage is primarily a loving and trusting relationship between a man and a woman who are also friends and companions. Christian marriage is that which must be lived in love and companionship. The real test of love comes when we are called to respond to the needs of the one we love. This type of love ought to be demonstrated in times of illness, and in time when care and attentions are needed. In love couple shares their being with each other. In this sharing of being each of the partners becomes a gift to the other. This gift is not an ordinary gift, it is a gift that must be appreciated and valued as a means of complementary of the being of the other. Christian marriage is a vocation to this companionship which couple forms with love as its primary foundation.

Man needs a woman in order to release and satisfy himself, even though he may also feel the impulse of love, strong or weak, genuine or imaginary. In like manner, the woman needs the man in order to awaken to herself to the fullness of her feminine self awareness. St Augustine calls the union of husband and wife in paradise a solid society founded on true love. This is a natural society of the different sexes, Arazu (1994).

Moreover, as a personal and communitarian act, the marriage contract is precisely (both an interpersonal and societal) covenant. It is a pact concluded between two persons and their respective clans (lineages) which are all concerned to give new opportunities to life, to love, to harmony, to peace and to security beyond their common frontiers of blood and ancestry. These covenants break down barriers between clan, nations, peoples and races and they endure even after the death of the two partners.

Furthermore, marriage that is well established in love creates an indelible mark of each other personality in the heart of either partner. This implies that even after death this love between the partners endures. A true Christian marriage is that which endures forever; first as a physical marriage which involves the presence of the two partners and secondary as spiritual marriage which involves the interaction of the two spirits of the living couple and the dead couple. Marriage indeed is a true companionship between two people of opposite sexes. This companionship involves self emptiness of either partner to the other in order to create room for harmonious existence.

However, a marriage that is not built on love is not a Christian marriage. This is because this marriage is never adaptable; it can easily be pulled by an ill wind. Marriage requires the fullest possible availability of the spouses to each other and their family. The true meaning of intercourse belongs to the intimate relationship of this marriage. Marriage gives room for an interaction of personalities, a testing of views, a trustworthy communication about one's feelings and views and all genuine friendships endow a mutual enrichment.

Obviously, the true mark of a Christian marriage is to ensure that what belongs to either of the partner's dignity is not to be denied.

Thus time, availability, new experiences, concern and affection which belong to the intimate relationship of marriage must not be reduced to the psychological detriment of either partner.

4.7 THE CHALLENGES OF CHRISTIAN MARRIAGE IN AFRICA

The incorporation of Christian marriage into an existing African culture often poses a threat to culture where marriage is seen as communitarian. Marriage in an Igbo culture is an ancestral task reserved for individual. This task is not performed personally but with the consent of parents and the extended family. On thc othcr hand Christian marriage is a personal decision taken from the innermost heart to accept the sharing of the being of the other irrespective of the up and down crisis of life. This is not the decision of the community. Christian marriage is a personal responsibility of the couple.

Nevertheless, Christian marriage seems to despise the communitarian hierarchy in projecting the will of the couple. In view of this there is always a conflict between the Christian marriage and the traditional understanding of marriage. The father in all attempt to impose his will on the child on the man or woman to marry, questions the Christian religion if his decision as the father is not honored. The

Christian marriage is a search for an authentic love. This type of love could only be found on personal will.

Furthermore, childlessness is often a challenge to the Christian marriage; where child bearing is not essential to the survival of the union. In occasions of childlessness, the Igbo tradition continues to question the authenticity of Christian marriage. Moreover, for the Igbo people, there is a continuity, which gives the soul-the undying part of the human person- a hold on immortality through the stages of life. This continuity is maintained through procreation, which is so considered as Sacred, and hence has a great place in social values. The underlying fact is that in the act of procreation, the living, the dead and the future generation, come together in conformity with the order of nature of which one's own life is part and an extension. And so, this attitude towards procreation under girds the practice of marriage to many wives, widow inheritance among others. In a situation of childlessness, it affects the stability of this sacred union standing in an Igbo culture.

The Igbo man often comes up with the adage; ***"no man is an island"***. In view of this, the continual questioning of the meaning of Christian marriage amidst childlessness causes the couple to rethink. The traditional marriage permits polygamous family. Sequel to this, the infidelity of a partner is consoled by the introduction of another wife. The Christian marriage becomes challenged in the act of infidelity. As the Christian tries to maintain the relationship of one wife, the traditional setting, frowns at this, and exerts pressure on the couple and consequently drives the man into polygamous marriage.

The equality shared between partners of Christian marriage becomes challenge to the traditional man, where the husband must continue to assert his will. The equality enjoyed by the Christian marriage is often being threatened by traditional belief that the man must be the dictator of the family. The more the Christian couple remains silent about it, the more the traditional setting continues to dissociate themselves from the Christian couple. The couple is referred to as people who have derailed and needed to be guided.

Priests in Africa are confronted with some challenges. Sequel to this, they have to deal with marriage on three levels: the preparation of a young Christian couple for marriage, the settling of a marriage case before the baptism of one or both partners, and the regularizing of the irregular marriage situation of a baptized couple. The first case is comparatively rare; the second case, presents few inherent problems in view of the extensive concession made in favor of the faith, the third case, is perhaps becoming more and more frequent and constitutes a serious pastoral problem. The irregular situation may be customary marriage or it may be extra-marital union altogether.

Nevertheless, Christian marriage is often challenged by; incompatibility of the partners, financial crisis, inability to meet the expenses of a lavish church wedding, Shortes (1973:183). The Christian marriage is often challenged by financial crisis in Africa. When there is financial crisis the love that flows between partners continues to dwindle. This is because when this occasion is not controlled by faith the couple loses confidence for each other and seeks an external body for a possible solution. In some African communities, the cause of the financial crisis is attributed to wife who may be innocent about it, once this happens; it brings disunity to a marriage which was once united. Though the vow of Christian marriage is for better and for worse, this marriage situated in Igbo culture is often affected by an ill wind which creates opportunity for external interventions.

Moreover, in the case of infertility of the first wife in African tradition, polygamy becomes the solution. This is because the woman would rather prefer to answer first wife to being divorced. The Christian idea of marriage abhors; the marriage of the second wife. Additionally, polygamy ensures wealth and prestige in agricultural communities. Having many wives is a sign of the wealth needed to pay bride wealth for them; it is a source of wealth, since the wives worked to raise food. This right of polygamous family; a means of African wealth, growth of the family is denied by the Christian marriage. Christianity hindrance to polygamous family is revised and bounced on Christianity as its threat.

Furthermore, the practice of gender inequality in Africa often poses a threat to Christian marriage, where husband and wife ought to sit together and decide for the good of the family. To the Igbo man this is self condescension on the part of the husband who often feels superior to the wife. The Christian marriage is a life lived in equality by the two partners who see themselves as both human who deserve human dignity.

The woman demands care and affection from the husband and husband demands fidelity and love from the wife. In this situation where equality is practiced between the partners, the Christian marriage becomes the object of caricature for the traditional Igbo setting where the husband demands absolute loyalty from the wife who is just like a handmaid to him. Christian marriage is a vocation to companionship while the traditional marriage is a vocation to dominance and loyalty on the side of man and woman.

4.8 THE CHURCH'S REFLECTION ON MARRIAGE

Marriage is affirmed by the church as a sacrament. This implies that it is not an empty action, rather it is an action embedded with meanings. Hence marriage is not a human action; it is an action of Jesus Christ in the church (CCC1603). Sacraments in general are ritual signs which give grace to the person who receives them. Sequel to this, marriage becomes a medium through which a couple fully committed to each other receives grace. The church's understanding of the sacredness of marriage is founded on the creation account in Genesis; "The Lord said: it is not good that the man should be alone therefore a man leaves his father and his mother and clings to his wife and they become one flesh". (Gen 2:18, 24).

However, the Catholic marriage is between one man and one wife. It is necessary to be aware of the kinds of relationship that are incompatible with marriage. It is not just a question of adultery. A husband and a wife have a legitimate claim on each other's time, attention, and affection. This does not always happen automatically and may require self control and determination to keep the promises made on wedding day.

The catholic marriage is different from simply living together. John Paul II begins his exposition of church's teaching on marriage by pointing out that, because human beings are created in the image of God who is love, the fundamental vocation of every human is to love. Since human persons are bodily, their bodies must share in love as they realize their vocation in one of two specific ways: marriage and virginity or celibacy. He then draws conclusion:

> "...sexuality, by means of which man and woman give themselves to one another through the acts which are proper and exclusive to spouses, is by no means something purely biological, but concerns the innermost being of the human person as such, it is realized in a truly human way only if it is an integral part of the love by which a man and a woman commit themselves totally to one another until death" (*Familiaris Consortio N.11*).

Thus marriage is not co-habitation. It is life lived by two persons harmoniously in love as one body whose aspirations is to reflect the love Christ has for the church. In Catholic marriage, partners exchange vows with each other, make solemn promises that are binding for the whole of their life. The exchange of vows is a sign of the work of Jesus Christ who joins in the unbreakable bond of marriage. The vows made to a partner during wedding can never be made to another while both partners are still alive.

The companionship involved in marriage cannot be achieved outside of marriage. The unconditional lifelong commitment made in marriage make it quite different from just living together. It is important to realize this and to be well prepared for it. Jesus broadens the Hebrew concept of marriage; he stood firmly on the oneness that exists between the man and the woman. The woman is not to be deserted at will. He emphasizes on divorce. Jesus strongly discouraged divorce and for Christ no man should divorce his wife at will. Hence, for one who marries a divorced woman commits adultery (Mt 5:31-32), McBrien (1994).

The advent of second Vatican council brought in modification with regard to marriage. Marriage was no longer seen as a contract as had traditionally viewed; instead the council speaks of marriage covenant which is sealed by an irrevocable personal consent (Pastoral Constitution on the Church in Modern World, n.48).

Furthermore, the council did not continue with the idea of projecting procreation as the most important aim of marriage as had earlier believed. Hence, the council advocated for mutual love of the couple. The council advises the couple to co-operate courageously with the love of the creator and savior who through them expands and enriches his own family (n.50).

Moreover, the council stresses that marriage is not just a ceremony by which two people are legally bound together. As sacrament, it is a mode of worship, an expression of faith, a sign of the church's unity, a mode of Christ's presence. The council adopted the term "christifideles". Marriage is not just a union between baptized Christians; it is a union between faithful Christians. Marriage once consummated by a single act of physical union can never be dissolved not even by Pope. Marriage involves the good of the whole person *(n.49, Humanae Vitae, 1968 n.8-9)*

The church emphasizes that it is well known anguish for a Christian marriage to breakdown. In view of this couple should reflect before committing themselves in marriage. It is quite pertinent that a good preparation should be made in doing this one lays a good foundation for a happy life together. The aim of human life is to learn how to love. In this world, nothing is more sacred than our relationship with others. The most precious moments in our life are those in which we have shared a close communion with someone else.

Chapter Five

Evaluation

5.1 EVALUATION OF CHRISTIAN MARRIAGE IN AFRICAN CULTURE

Christian marriage has often encountered tremendous problems in Igbo dominating areas. The reason for this remains the cultural orientation of the Africans, which differs greatly from the Christian outlook. Igbo traditional marriage remains a communitarian event where the consents of the couple, themselves, is not significant as compared to the extended family in which the new marriage will be established. Christianity is a religion of freedom; it therefore permits individuals freewill through which, they become responsible for their actions.

Christian marriage therefore confers enormous importance to the couple who will be engaged in marriage. It therefore means no marriage will be valid if the consent of the partners of the marriage is not honored. In view of this, the question remains: can Christian marriage survive in this culture, where marriage is in the hand of the community, women are subordinated and the couple significance is reduced?

5.2 KINSHIP RELATION IN AFRICA: IT'S EFFECT ON CHRISTIAN MARRIAGE

Marriage among the Africans is communitarian, thus it is the responsibility of kin groups. The importance and role of the family in the traditional Igbo society cannot be overemphasized. The family remains the nucleus of the society and everything tends to revolve around the family. For this very reason the family is considered sacred in this society. This means that the hierarchical structure of the family has to be religiously preserved. In view of the significance attached to the family ties and kinship in Igbo Traditional society,

Kinship affiliation becomes a factor which plays a prominent role in the Igbo marriage.

Marriage among the Igbo people is the alliance between two kin groups. It follows that marriage is not so much the affair of two individuals; it is mainly the concern of the groups in which the marriage partners belong. The family is a source of one's pride and honor; hence there is a strong recommendation for one to be affiliated to his family for full recognition in the society. To uproot one from one's family or to find oneself foreign to one's family is viewed as a serious misfortune. Among the Igbo people it is appropriate for the father to choose the daughter's husband and also the woman the man wants to marry should be the one the extended family approves Moore (1968).

African kinship is often a challenge to Christian marriage. This is not incredible, in African kinship the responsibility of marriage and love is left for the wider circle of kindred and thus the husband loses that direct responsibility and love for the wife. Christian marriage is a vocation of love in which a man or a woman willfully or consciously chooses a man or a woman of his or her choice. In Igbo cultural settings this task is left for the kindred, who are the custodians of marriage.

Furthermore, in this kinship influence, the newly married wife is the spouse of all. In this large circle of influence, the woman is jealously guided by all. In trying to guard the woman, she becomes over supervised and she loses the power of assertion. The principle of over vigilance is not favorable to Christian marriage, in order to attain inner development and mutual understanding so as to strengthen the marriage.

The heart of any Igbo society is the family and the center in which human existence can gain its full development is the kindred. The kindred are made up of many families who are related by common ancestor. These members of the kindred play prominent role in African marriage.

However, African family is not conceived the way family is conceived in the western terms. African family ties are more often thought of as categorical than individual. Indeed, most terms of relationship are applied not to the individual but to a group of persons. Thus all members of the same generation within a group of relations, or group regarded as relations may call each other brothers and sisters.

Furthermore, this family system of the Igbo people, which forms its kinship, plays a significant role in marriage. Marriage is not an affair of a man neither is it a personal affair of the woman. It is a condition which is initiated and approved by the extended family. This is because any marriage is a contribution to the building up of the family strength. Sequel to this, marriage becomes the affair of the family.

5.3 THE FUTURE OF CHRISTIAN MARRIAGE IN THE KINSHIP ORIENTED ENVIRONMENT

Christian marriage projects love independent on material acquisition, procreation or physical beauty; it is not marriage that is interested on the physical beauty and physique, but that, which penetrates into the essence of humanity. It is the sacrificial act which God himself created ; of a man and a woman living together, sharing their experiences, their joys, their sorrows, helping one another, supporting one another, working together, sojourning in life, possible also, looking after their family, predominantly sharing the reality of their experience. When this love is sincerely expressed in Christian marriage it becomes cherished by the traditional African man.

Furthermore, for Christian marriage to be sustainable, it should not be isolated from the rest of the kins that edifies the Igbo community. Hence, the Christian couples should develop a cordial relationship with the kins, which form the extended family of both man and the woman. In relating with the kins, the Christian couple communicates the priority to the world, this is selfless love; a love which demands dying for the other. In exhibiting this attitude to the world, Christian marriage becomes a model even in the traditional setting.

Nevertheless, Christian couple needs to remind themselves that people are more important than possessions. They should consider friendliness and hospitality to people around as essential factors in order to promote a better rapport with people around Foley (1981). The Christian couple should understand that it is not what they have in the society that counts but how they relate with the society in which they live. In marriage there is nothing more important than relationship with others around.

Furthermore, marriage couple should see the family as the church in miniature, through its mutual love, its common prayer, and its work for social justice. The family should be a place of relief for those who are homeless. Marriage provides couple with a unique opportunity of fulfilling the basic aims of Christianity which is to live a life of love and service to the people. The demands, which marriage makes on our time, the restrictions it makes or our privacy, the limitations it can have on our personal freedom are all aspects of this.

Christian marriage opens the mind to have a feel of the eschatological world. It is in this union that the love of Christ for the church is experienced by those who are involved. It is the nursery bed of any society. For Christian marriage to linger and raised to the standard, couple should develop the trust that comes with true intimacy in order to project to all, eschatological world that is lived here and now on earth.

However, for Christian marriage to fulfill its task of being a model to the world marriage relationship between the partners must have two basic characteristics: it must be based on exclusive faithfulness and it must be permanent. This permanence is based on the fact that no circumstance in life should obstruct the marital love and relationship.

As Christians, we are called to love everyone, but the special love we show for our married couple, which is sealed by our sexual union, is for our mutual benefit and support. If a man and woman are to grow in this love, they need the security of knowing that it is special to them. Although, sexual activity between married couples is a universal phenomenon, on a personal level, this intimate sharing has a unique equality, which sustains married couples because of this, unfaithfulness gnaw at the very foundation of marriage.

The Christian marriage should be christocentric, and this is the essence of this Christian union. If a marriage is founded on Christ and yearns toward Christ, many of the problems encountered in marital life today will be overcome. The Christian opposition; to divorce is based on Christ saying; "what God has joined together, let no man put asunder". Hence for Christian marriage to remain firm, it must be directed towards Christ. It is not just the partners' love which binds them, but the love of God, which the couple shares because their marriage is christocentric.

5.4 THE CHRISTIAN MARRIAGE AS A VOCATION

Marriage is a vocation. This is because this union is a call from God to share the love he shares with the world, which he demonstrated by the sacrificial death of his son. The church's teaching that marriage is a vocation is an emphasis that the couple's relationship is more than simply their choice to enter a union, which is social and legal institution. In addition to these things, marriage involves a call from God and a response from two people who promise to build, with the help of divine grace, a lifelong, intimate and sacramental partnership of love and life. Hence in marriage two distinct individuals not related by blood come together to live in mutual love and equality advocated by Christ (Gal 3:28).

Marriage is understood theologically as a permanent bond between one man and a woman. In this sense, marriage is seen as a vocation. The call to this bond which is permanent and irrevocable is a call to love "the fundamental and innate vocation of every human being". In vocation of marriage, something which is written in the very nature of man and woman, we see that, the love of husband and wife becomes an image of the absolute and unfailing love with which God loves.

A vocation is a personal call. It is offered freely and must be accepted freely. Attraction to a certain way of life or to a specific person can be a good sign of being call. Most often a person comes to recognize and accept a vocation gradually. This process, sometimes called discernment, is an opportunity for growth. It can be helped by prayer and guidance from trusted mentors, friends and family.

Scripturally speaking God is seen as the author of marriage. In Gen 2:18-25, we read that God said, "It is not good for man to be alone, I will make a suitable partner for him". God made woman out of man, and for that reason man leaves his father and mother and clings to his wife, and the two of them become one flesh. The biblical passage brings on board the divine institution of marriage. Marital life is a call by God to take responsibility expressed in the moral upbringing of children. In fact it is in exercising these day to day responsibilities that we help to build up the church, a task which the council says is common to all Christians.

Marriage involves an attraction of two individuals not related by blood. However, what begins as attraction must deepen into conviction and commitment. Those who are called to the married life should be ready to learn what their vocation means and acquire the virtues and skills needed for a happy and holy marriage. The family is indeed, a school for human enrichment, a center for human moral development and a domestic church. This is what God himself created; Christ continues to bless them. This is the source of the fundamental education. A peaceful family raises children that bring harmony and tranquility in the society (Vatican II: 956).

Married couple should see their marital status as task given to them by God to create a society of peace love and unity. Married couple should regard their union as mission to transmit human life and to educate their children. They should realize that they are thereby cooperating with the love of God the creator and in a certain sense its interpreter. The vocation to marriage is a call to a life of holiness and service within the couple's own relationship and in their family *(Constitution on the Church, N.40)*. As a particular way of following the Lord, this vocation also challenges a couple to live their marriage in a way that expresses God's truth and love in the world.

The family is the nursery bed of love, justice, peace, and unity. A couple that fails to inculcate these moral values in their children fails in the mission given to them by God. It therefore means that acceptance to join the marital life is the readiness to respond to the mission of God in bringing up children to live out the moral values.

However, the most basic reason for Christian marriage is to bring men and women out of their isolation and aloneness, so that they can complete or complement one another in a relationship of love. Hence in Gen 2:18 and the Lord GOD said; "It is not good that man should be alone, I will make him a helper comparable to him". The marriage and the family are the settings in which most people are called to holiness of life. Marriage as a vocation, which takes delight not just in procreation, but in honestly fulfilling this act of procreation and the achievement of the task of ensuring the education and moral upbringing of children, Arazu (1994).

5.5 CHRISTIAN MARRIAGE: RESISTANT TO SOCIAL CHALLENGES

For Christian marriage to remain a model, it must be distinct from other marriages in traditional African setting. In maintaining this distinctiveness, Christian marriage must accommodate or accept social problems as conditions of life, inevitable, once is determined by God. In expressing this resistance, Christian marriage must be able to withstand economic instability, health failure, political instability, cultural biases and gossips.

In the time of economic crisis, Christian marriage or families should be instrument of consolation to others. Hence, Christianity perceives the world as not a bed of roses neither is it a bed of thorns. So then, when economy fluctuates, the couple should be able to understand that no situation in life is permanent, that it is only God by virtue of his divine nature who is permanent. In time of crisis couples should develop mutual understanding of one another. The presence of any of the partners amidst these challenges of life is often a source of consolation, hope and victory. Successes and failures are often championed by the human minds. This implies that with determination and well disposition of the mind, successes in life becomes accessible to the Christian couple just at the tip of their hands.

The failure of the health of one partner is not the termination of Christian marriage, rather in this condition the authenticity of this sacred union is expressed vividly. Hence St Paul says explicitly (Eph 5) that marriage is and should be in a certain way an image and echo of the love between Christ and the church. Marriage and covenant between God and humanity in Christ can only be compared by us, they stand objectively in such a relation that matrimony objectively represents this love of Christ for the church, Rahner (1963). In view of this love experienced in Christian marriage which echoes the love of Christ for us, Christian marriage often remains resistant to up and down of life, health and ill-health.

Furthermore, political instability could be a threat to marital life; this is because certain principles in the family may be affected by the political laws of a state. Wife and husband relationship may be influenced by the politics of a given nation. In time of political instability there arise problems on the mode of husband-wife relationship. Christian marriage takes Christ as a model in his relationship with the church. Hence, the sacred union is not affected by political instability, since the mutual love that exists between the couple is established by God himself. Since God is the beginning and focus of marital life, the Christian marriage remains a distinctive institution since it is divinely established. The ill-wind that does no one good is often counteracted by the unconditional love of Christian marriage.

Christian marriage is never moved by cultural biases or sentiments such as OSU caste system, tribalism, favoritism and so on. This is based on the ground that we are all God's children. This follows the principle that humanity shares equality with one another. The death and resurrection of our Lord Jesus Christ has made us equal before God. But through the resurrection of Christ, man is liberated from the bondage of sin. The sacred bond of marriage does not depend on human criticism; neither does it depend on human decision alone. For God himself is the author of marriage and has endowed it with various benefits and with various ends in view *(Gaudium et Spes No. 48).*

Chapter Six

Conclusion

6.1 SUMMARY

Marriage is a sacred union, instituted by God. This union involves two persons donating themselves to each other; in order to enjoy the fullness of humanity in a life lived in companionship and trust. This institution can experience disintegration when it is devoid of the virtues of patience, love, selflessness, understanding, ideological sharing and sacrifice. When this union is lived in mutual understanding and in symbiotic relationship, spouses begin to appreciate the being of each other and the marital love is increased with the bond of marriage being strengthened.

However, care should be taken in this relationship, so that the personality of each other will not be destroyed in anger, careless use of words, infidelity and impatience. Impatience is a great virus to marital love. When it is allowed to reign in marriage it affects the bond of marriage, destroys marital love and consequently leads to disintegration. Communication is a virtue that must be cultivated by spouses. It is through this means that spouses empty each other being before the other who is a being of consciousness.

The virtues of Christian marriage should be cultivated in Igbo traditional setting. These are the virtues of selflessness, total commitment, love, patience and steadfastness in any condition of life. However, the Christian marriage should emulate some virtues in Igbo marriage. These are the virtues of communal spirit, which draws couple to the community and remain attentive to her community, because of the consciousness of her, being the foundation of marriage, also the virtue of loyalty; the loyalty not only to the husband but between the spouses. Christian couple should understand that no man is an island; with regard to this spouses should be extensive in their relationship. Kinship is a valuable factor that must not be despised. The happiness of any marriage is being increased by the support of kinship.

Nevertheless, Christian marriage should be ready and disposed to project to the world, that which sustains every marriage. This is love; a virtue, which binds the master Jesus with the church, the Lord and Savior of Christianity. The fact that marriage is transformational must not be neglected by spouses. This is because as spouses advance in age, they begin to perceive the world differently in more deeper and reflective way. In a situation like this, the perception of marriage begins to change. In most cases, spouses begin to appreciate each other better.

Conflict is inevitable in any healthy marriage. This must be managed with greater level of maturity in order to reach a resolution. Third parties are dangerous to marital unity, they are not needed in all conflict resolutions or else they change the structure of the marriage and create a scar that remains indelible in the mind of the spouses. Resolutions are achieved through patience, malleability, gentleness, love and selflessness.

Christian marriage is a vocation. This is because marriage is instituted by God and has a plan for humanity, which is to fill the earth and responsibility to nurture children following his lay down precepts, and thereby increasing morality in the world. The acceptance of marriage is an agreement to respond to this divine responsibility positively, thereby renewing the face of the earth.

The Christian marriage is not a contradiction to the traditional marriage. The fact remains that no culture is perfect; it is in comparison that a better society is built. As Christian marriage projects its virtue of steadfastness, love and sacrifice, the traditional marriage projects its virtue of communal solidarity. It is in mingling of these ideological differences that a perfect and sustainable marriage is achieved.

The marital life is fortified when couple realizes that the union, in which they are involved, is divinely instituted. The recognition of this divine authorship of marriage should influence couple in their relationship with one another, in achieving a sustainable marriage, transparent in its expression of love. Marital partners should acknowledge that they are gifts to each other and therefore be ready to be opened to each other.

Love must be demonstrated in marriage, practically through the couple sharing of ideas, communication and readiness to die for each other. The real marital life begins, when couple begins to understand that each other exists for the good of the other and cannot be complete without the collaboration of the other partner. Couple should be disposed to thank each other for their mutual presence. They can say with or without words, thank you for being here, I am grateful for your presence yesterday and today, Dominian (1981). Below are recommendations for a successful marriage.

6.2 CONTRIBUTIONS TO KNOWLEDGE

This is an exposition of what marriage should be considering its challenges in life. It is an eye opener to a life commitment, in which the consent of partners involved must be sought and respected. Even though marriage has a communitarian effect, it must not be imposed by the community to the individual, since it is a life experienced more closely by the spouses themselves. This project is a challenge to every Tom, Dick and Harry, that marriage is not just a mere mundane celebration; it is a life full of mortifications, self donation to the other and a sharing of being.

Moreover, it enlightens the mind that marriage is not only affirmation of love but a demonstration of love in a life lived in companionship, which involves dying for the growth and development of the other. Hence, it is an education to the world that the two individuals of different temperament, biological constitution and emotional state can live together, once there is an understanding, developed by a mutual love. Thus marriage is a symbiotic relationship; where each is a gift for the other for his completeness in life and for the realization of his goals, taking into consideration that in marriage man reaches his fullness of humanity.

Furthermore, this project reminds us that in marriage the two partners are equal to each other. The two partners share their being together, each needs the other, a spouse is incomplete except he unites with the other and enjoys the fullness of humanity. It is a shared responsibility between equals who understand themselves, love each other and promote the good of either spouse. It is a life lived in companionship bound by love and enjoys the fruit, which is the joy of a new born baby.

Nevertheless, this paper calls to mind that marriage is a life initiated by two, who have a social task of regenerating the community. In view of this marriage is a social and individual task. Though the society enjoys the benefits of marriage, should allow spouses to make voluntary choices to marriage, hence marriage is a freely undertaken venture, taken up with courage, demonstrated in love, lived in sacrifice of self donation and strengthened by the fear of God. This implies that marriage is a vocation of courage, love, sacrifice and fear of God. When these factors are excluded from marriage, it becomes a co-habitation lived in fear and aggressiveness.

When marriage is established, a miniature symbiotic community is established, where partners come together to exchange their being for the good of each spouse, for the purpose of creating a new and independent individual capable of reason. The new child is the fruit of the love of the couple. Childlessness, however, is not an indication of the cessation of marriage but challenges the fundamental task of marriage; which is love.

Enduring love attracts God's mercy; it opens up a way for a better understanding of each other. Marriage in itself is an exclusive relationship in which a man and a woman commit themselves to each other in covenant for life and on the basis of this solemn vow become one flesh physically(Gen 2:24, Mal 2:14).

6.3 MARRIAGE ENHANCEMENT

I COMMUNICATION: A WAY OF IMPROVING MARRIAGE

Communication is an essential factor in marriage. Communication is a means, through which the identity of a partner is revealed to the other, this is usually through conveying inner needs to each other and re-assessing the mutual understanding of each other. In communication the wound of the past is unraveled and through this, healing is achieved. When communication becomes deficient the identity of spouses becomes hidden and this creates tension and impedes the flow of love intrinsic to Christian marriage.

Emotional communication holds a central place in the relationship of the spouses. The couple needs to feel recognized, wanted and appreciated at other times than when they are having sexual intercourse. This caring revolves round acknowledgement, which is expressed in appropriate communication. There are plenty of everyday activities, which need caring communication. Couples may have different rhythms of activity and rest and so times of going to bed and rising may need adjustment. Some want a really warm bed and other find heat unbearable. The times meal are taken and the type of food may clash. Above all, the time spent together and the time each needs the other has to be structured. All these arrangements are being expressed in communication.

Obviously, through communication spouses empty each other self for the other, by revealing innermost feelings and inclinations to the other, which when hidden may be detrimental to marital life. It is quite obvious that eager, happiness, sorrow and anxiety are expressed through communication. When these are expressed vocally, it grants internal healing to the spouses and enhances mutual understanding to each other's personality. Marriage without communication, often experiences a bitter breakdown, an explosive anger, which its consequence, could be detrimental to the continuity of an established marriage.

Communication can be verbal, physical, social, emotional, intellectual or spiritual. Husbands and wives talk and listen, touch and respond, make love, socialize and act as a group, express and receive affection, exchange ideas and give spiritual acknowledgement of each other. What is important in marriage is that a couple feels and knows that they trust and can reach other in whatever communication suits them best.

Moreover, sexual communion needs preparation, which in turn needs adequate communication between the spouses. Each has to tell the other what they enjoy in the phase of foreplay. They need to convey information about appearance, touch, stroking, caressing, kissing and the time needed to arouse both partners. Good communication is thus essential; spouses should not be frightened to reveal their real sexual desires in case they are rejected, rather they should be proud to communicate their sexual state. This is because; through this communication marital relationship is strengthened.

II SELFLESSNESS: KEY TOWARDS UNDERSTANDING THE OTHER

Marriage was an intention of God; to be a beautiful relationship and to be a great fulfillment for men and women. In marriage, God wishes a perfect union and affection, edification, satisfaction and fulfillment between a man and a woman. In the midst of selfishness, this divine plan for marriage will not be fruitful and it only becomes an utopia. There is no room in marriage for selfishness. Instead every marriage should be dominated by selflessness in order for the ideal of marriage to be materialized. Hence selflessness needs to be the cornerstone of marriage.

No wonder Apostle Paul gave us Philip 2:3, "Let nothing be done through strife or vainglory, but in lowliness of mind, let each esteem other better than themselves". This verse ought to be hanging in every home and we should constantly remind ourselves of this directive of the Apostle Paul, for if everyone in every marriage follows these directions, then we would have heaven on earth. Marriage involves a constant sacrifice of constant readiness to accepting the other the way he or she is and to influence the other positively, when need arises, without the destruction of the personality of the other. However, in every successful marriage, there ought to be three components of selflessness. They all begin with "M" for Maturity, Magnanimity, and Malleability.

MATURITY: In maturity a spouse thinks on how to satisfy his or her spouse with his or her limited resources, instead of thinking on how he or she will be satisfied by his or her spouse. In doing this, one donates himself or herself freely to his or her spouse. Maturity says; "how can I be more patient with my spouse in spite of his or her flaw". On the contrary, immaturity only thinks of the self and neglects the responsibility to the other. Hence, immaturity thinks on how well it can be satisfied in spite of the unfavorable condition of the spouse. It does not think of the good of the spouse but thinks about itself. Maturity is a very necessary ingredient to selflessness which is a great and sustaining pillar of a Blessed Marriage.

Furthermore, the principle of **Magnanimity** involves a generous self donation to the other. It comprises of being generous in forgiving, eschewing resentment or revenge, unselfishness. Magnanimity is ingredient to selflessness. Magnanimity is the opposite of insensitivity.

Let us see what the Bible says about this word, that is not there in the scripture but the meaning is there; "Wherefore be you not unwise, but understanding what the will of the Lord is" (Eph 5:17). The sentence implies magnanimity means seeking to understand my spouse thought and feelings and needs. Magnanimity means to study the person so well that no wonder the apostle Peter says, "Live with your wife according to knowledge". In First Peter 3:7, this study is not easy. It is hardwork, but it can be fulfilling, especially as you see the progress you make from one stage to the next. Study of your wife needs and feelings are not easy, especially when they conflict with your needs. But the alternative to understanding is foolishness and who wants that.

Another component to selflessness is **Malleability**. By dictionary definition, it is a noun meaning the property of something that can be worked or hammered or shaped under pressure without breaking. It is the ability to adjust to changing circumstances; adaptability. Hence, the bottom line of malleability implies that husband and wife, some more or to a lesser degree, submits to one another, for Jesus' sake. Malleability means, that each sacrifices for the other. Stubbornness is the opposite of malleability, and stubbornness is a characteristic of sin.

Nevertheless, the above analysis does not imply; no disagreement. It means that because of maturity, magnanimity and malleability you are going to have selflessness in marriage and when there is the cornerstone of selflessness, there will be a blessed marriage.

III PATIENCE: KEY TO SUCCESSFUL MARRIAGE

One should try to understand his partner as best as he or she can. Hence, one should be ready to draw oneself in place of one's partner for a better assimilation of the other. Drawing oneself close to another, means relating to the other partner; both intellectually and emotionally with greater and deeper expression of love. The attainment of this intimacy becomes impossible without patience, as patience is the facilitator to this social movement to the other.

As one comes closer to one's partner with the power of patience, one's perspective towards his partner begins to change and the positive side of one's partner begins to glitter. One begins to see his or her partner in a more favorable light and even to recognize that apparent blemishes he or she had observed in one's partner are actually reflections of identical, though less apparent, blemishes in himself.

With patience careful planning is achieved, hardwork is encouraged and dedication becomes visible, in service to each other in marriage.

Marriage involves the relationship of two, who become one under the imperative of the Christian marriage. The union of these two, with different temperaments, is often difficult, without the power of patience. The interaction of two or more people is often encountered with anger, intolerance, aggressiveness, depression and despondency. Patience is the antidote to anger. With regard to others in general and one's spouse in particular one must strive to assume the divine attribute of "infinite Patience".

Infinite Patience is the consciousness, the infinite broad "space" of mind which fosters one's ability to wait for conflict to resolve itself, to suspend judgment to continuously check and control one's innate tendency to relate to others impulsively. Patience is the key to avoiding damage, one inflicts upon oneself and others when unable to control the responses of his "first nature" to life situation.

Man in a state of nature is self inclined according to Thomas Hobbes (1473-1543). In this state of nature, people are capable of hurting their neighbors' and taking what they need for their own protection.

Differences in strength can lead to terrorism; the strong can destroy the weak, Stumpf (1994). Patience is the virtue that challenges man in his natural state. Hence through patience, spouses begin to consider the needs of their partners and begin the business of self donation. With patience one understands the weakness and strength of the other and considering them as variables of life, which aids in perfect complementarities of life.

Both marriage partners need to be constantly vigilant in cultivating patience. Patience depends upon faith and trust in God. If we want something and do not receive it, it is because we do not yet sufficiently deserve it. When spouses realize this, they become much more patient with each other. Rather than demanding that their partner be more perfect than themselves, their focus will be on rectifying their own character first, with the help of God.

With patience, comes the ability of a spouse to donate oneself freely to the other. Hence, through patience one transcends one's innate mortal character and fulfils the commandment to emulate God. Just as God is merciful, so should spouses be merciful to each other. Just as he is infinitely patient, so should partners cultivate infinite patience in the relationship with each other.

Authenticity in patience engenders awareness that God is ever present in one's reality and influencing one through his will and providence. This awareness of the reality of God in the other draws one to the other, mobilizes one to listen to the other with care and attention and with ultimate patience. Patience is that which keeps one in hope that nothing is constant. What appears bad today could turn good tomorrow; a bad behavior can be refined with gentle approach. Patience is that, which sees beyond the physical appearance of the other and does not stick to the present, but wait hopefully for a brighter future.

Nevertheless, from the above analysis, it becomes vivid that infinite patience is the key to successful marriage. In patience, a spouse succeeds in rectifying the attributes of his or her own soul, having integrated infinite patience into his or her life; it then begins to influence the life of its spouse through sweet and gentle words. Remember, the words of the wise, when spoken gently are harkened (Eccl 9:17).

IV CONFLICT AND RESOLUTION: FACTORS OF HEALTHY MARRIAGE

Conflict is that which is inevitable in any marriage. But resolution is that, which is only possible through maturity of the mind. For every conflict there is a great expectation for a resolution, this is a product of love and selflessness. Disagreement can be a very healthy vehicle to promote expansiveness of vision and personal growth. The real secret to a good and lasting marriage is not lack of conflict, but how conflict is resolved. In order to achieve resolutions in conflicts that emanate among spouses, they should learn not to generalize and should face the immediate problem as an isolated problem. Hence, when disagreeing, words like; "you always do that" should be avoided. Such broad sweeping generalization could be very damaging. No one is always wrong. No one always behaves negatively, and it obscures the issue at hand putting the accused party on the defensive.

Moreover, just as with our children we want to avoid the destructive use of labels, so we do in marriage as well. And just as with our children, we want to bolster self esteem with a lot of praises before alluding to a potential area for improvement, so couples do with their marriage partners also. We would not attack our children over a mistake they made, so also should spouses show respect to each other.

Spouses should learn to use a gentle tone of voice. This is the voice that shows care, love and self surrendering to each other. I think the whole world would change for the better, if everyone would learn how to speak softly. Your spouse, your children, your friends and colleagues, even animals, respond much more positively to a request or complaint expressed in a soft and gentle manner. You could say the same thing loudly with much less effects and frequently, create a hostile atmosphere. Speak pleasantly and softly when you admonish your spouse, it is an expression of love.

A calm gentle approach protects the ego of the person and allows him or her to hear the rebuke more objectively. We, sometimes feel that in order to be heard we need to be loud, maybe we need to yell and scream. This is a common mistake and a dangerous virus to marriage. If you speak calmly, there is a much lesser chance of your discussion deteriorating into a brawl. Even if your spouse is a screamer, your gentle tones will stop him in his tracks and force him to calm down too, and it is a great example to set for your children.

Nevertheless, it is very helpful when you are in middle of a rough spot in your marriage and the door looks pretty tempting, to take a look inside yourself. What have you been telling yourself? Is it true or an exaggeration? Is there a more positive way you could put this? Does everyone else in the world really have a better husband/ wife/

mother in-law? Could you deal with your frustration and affirm your marriage at the same time. What we tell ourselves, the tape we play is crucial to how we look at and handle each challenging situation in our marriage.

However, for resolution to be achieved, if you have criticism to offer, try to precede it with a positive comment. Loud personal attacks are embarrassing and humiliating for both the attacker and the victim. Instead of demonstrating to your spouse with the expression; "I cannot stand it", try; "I think I can, I think I can". When such discipline is developed for every conflict a resolution will be achieved without the destruction of each other personality and a healthy and sustainable marriage is assured.

6.4 SUGGESTIONS FOR FURTHER RESEARCH

Though there is a great effort by the researcher to explore deeply into the contemporal challenges of marriage today, this project is handicapped by the stipulated number of pages and thus unable to exhaust the entire challenges of marital life. This project only provides essential areas needed to establish a sustainable marriage. It therefore serves as a catalyst for further researches on related topics such as;

1. Human Temperament: An inevitable factor for Good Marriage.

2. Environment an agent for sustainable marriage.

3. Roles of Government in marriage.

4. Sexual Education: Foundation for Sustainable Marriage.

References

Adjaero, N. M., (1996), *The Structure of the Family: A Social Institution,* Enugu: Spiritan Publications.

Agbasiere, J. T., (2000), *Women in Igbo Life and Thought*, New York: Taylor and Francis Group.

Adegbola, E.A., (1983), *Traditional Religion in West Africa,* Ibadan: Daystar Press.

Arazu, R., (1994), *Covenant Broken and Reconciliation,* Enugu: Liz Press Services Ltd.

Benezeri, K., et.el, (1977), *African Christian Marriage,* Nairobi, Kenya: Paulines Publication Africa.

Dennehy, R., (1981), *Christian Married Love,* U.S.A: Ignatius Press.

Dominian, J., (1981), *Marriage, Faith and Love,* London: Darton, Longman and Todd Ltd.

Dontan, T. C., (1983), *Towards Marriage in Christ,* Dubuque, Iowa: The Prior Press.

Edeh, E., (1985), *Towards an Igbo Metaphysics,* Chicago: Loyola University Press.

Foley, M., (1981), *Marriage a Relationship, Preparation and Fulfilment.* London: The Anchor Press Ltd.

James, G., (1993), *Creating a Marriage,* New York: Paulist Press.

Jean P.B., (1987), *How to Understand Marriage,* New York: The Crossroad Publishing Company.

Mary S. C., M.D and Eric W. Johnson, (1989), *The Family Book About Sexuality,* New York: Harper and Row Publishers.

McBrien, R. P. (1994), *Catholicism,* New York: Harper SanFrancisco.

Moore, C. D., (1968), *African Yesterday and Today.*

Rahner, K., (1963), *The Church and Sacraments.* London: Search Press Ltd.

Schillebeeckx E., (1965), *Marriage Human Reality and Saving Mystery,* Great Britain, Sheed and Ward LTD.

Shorter, A. W., (1973), *Africa Culture and the Christian Church.* London: Geoffrey Chapman.

Stumpf, S. E., (1994), *Philosophy, History and Problems.* U.S.A: McGraw-Hill, Inc.

Thomas, D. M., (1983), *Christian Marriage: A Journey Together.* U.S.A: Michael Glazier, Inc.

Thomas, E. J., (1977), *Marital Communication and Decision Making.* London: The Free Press.

www.ingramcontent.com/pod-product-compliance
Ingram Content Group UK Ltd.
Pitfield, Milton Keynes, MK11 3LW, UK
UKHW040559210726
13854UKWH00008B/1549

9 781504 946933